My Solace

A poem collection

Sakshi Singh

 pencil

ISBN 978-93-5610-797-7
© Sakshi Singh 2022
Published in India 2022 by Pencil

A brand of

One Point Six Technologies Pvt. Ltd.
123, Building J2, Shram Seva Premises,
Wadala Truck Terminal, Wadala (E)
Mumbai 400037, Maharashtra, INDIA
E connect@thepencilapp.com
W www.thepencilapp.com

Author biography

Sakshi is a teenage girl who loves to write.
When she writes she wants her readers to experience every emotion which she felt while writing.Apart from writing she likes boxing, reading and many other stuffs.

CONTENTS

Death

Where will I go when I die?
Down below in Hell or up in the sky?
Or will I become a star and shine,
Or will I roam in the woods and haunt people at night?
Death knows I won't stop for him,
So one day death will stop for me instead.
I know my life will pass like the trances of a cloud.
And a piece of your abandoned heart will not be answered
With my words in sound.

Paradise

I want to live in paradise,
A world where there is only light.
I want to touch clouds with my finger tips,
I want to visit deity's garden during spring.

I want to be free from cycle of life and death,
But I also want to help people with my existence.
I want to see paradise and the great deities with my eyes.

The one who dies, sees the paradise
This is the misconception of many people in my life.
Heaven and Hell are both inside you,
That's what I think.
All you have to do is listen to your soul
And you will feel it.

Sound of Heart

Each first time is an adventure, with destination unknown.
Expecting the unexpected and embracing it
will let you know,
about the journey which is yours.

Like a tree in a deserted land,
I am firm and all alone.,
Waiting for someone to come and cherish,
Waiting for someone who knows my worth.

Just like a bird in a golden cage,
My emotions are trapped somewhere far away.
Roaming in a cold world,
I am looking for a warm place.

Night sky

When the moon glows in the darkness of the sky
many things which were forgotten are remembered in that
light.,
Doesn't matter how far the sun is,
I just know only one thing that you are mine.
Maybe I don't know how to express my feelings,
but I still like counting stars because it reminds me of
us when we were thirteen.
No matter how far I have came,
No matter how much I have gain.,
But I am still occupied with my leo constellation and stars
in the sky.
I have seen Ursa Major many times but
'Aquarius - the water carrier is mine.'
Aquarius is refered to sea in the region of the sky because
it contains number of constellation such as Eridanus,
Cetus and Pisces in the night sky.
No matter what our age is but when we look in the night
sky it tells us our problems are not that tough as it seems
like.
When again the moon will glow in the darkness of the sky,
many things which were forgotten will be remembered in
that night light.

Imprint of heart

I am emotionless , that's what I show
But how much I feel the pain only my pillow knows.
There are nights, I don't sleep
Thinking about the past really makes me freeze.

I am somehow lost in a cold world, with emotions
I can't show to others.
I wear a mask called confidence,
But deep down I am the most insecured human.
The thing about confidence is that no one knows,
whether it is real or fake and that helps me win the game.

A lot of emotions are up in my mind,
All screaming "choose me instead", "I am right".
Choosing an emotion is really complicated,
But for most of the time,
I am certain that 'Pain' is the name.

They say I have bottled up my emotions somewhere,
Maybe deep down in my heart where to go is prohibited.
Even when I cry , emotions are somewhere within me,
they do not come out as they are supposed to be.
Even crying does not help now, only tears pour down and
for emotions, I have to help myself a little more.

I want to open the bottle someday but yet it feels like a really long way.

Two faces

Everyday I try to fight for my happiness,
Everyday I fight with myself.
Everyday I want to die but two faces ,
two faces come near my eyes.
I don't know how much I can hold,
I don't know how long I will hold.
But I have to be strong because
I have a family to support and take care of.
Two faces that comes near my eyes,
everyday and every night,
I can't leave them crying behind

Separation

Death can't separate us because we have a special bond.
The body might become useless but ,love can't be replaced .,
Cause in this life I loved you the most ,from your heart to
your soul
Without direction ,without hope
It feels like somewhere I am lost.
Your eyes and your smile, has a print on my heart.
Even when I am not certain ,
For you I can still do that all.
The road seems winding with destination somewhere lost,
Sometimes anxious ,Sometimes fawning.
I'm still holding dreams because you are there for me,
And I can see you supporting.
Looking at the stars, I can see your smile
No matter where you are you'll always be mine.
Cause You were the one I loved the most in this world
which is really cold

Chance

I also need a chance, to move forward and shine like a star.
I do also need love because I too have feelings that hurt.
I also don't like lonliness , because I know it sucks.
I also want a hug , because I know it gives comfort.
Life is not about running first but its about coming first.
So, I also need a chance to move forward and shine like a
star.

A Feeling

Everyone has a time when they are tired of everything,
Just want to drop everything and run.
That time will come to you
And I will face that moment too.

We will know each other on the way of life,
But for now I want you to wipe the tears and smile.

Everyone wants to convey something ,
Deep down in their hearts, A feeling hidden somewhere in
the dark.
Maybe I can tell you now,
about the uncertain situation of my heart.

Keep weaving dreams with hope and kindness,
And once you wipe your tears away,
Your smile will become my light.

Pain

The pain in your eyes tells a lot,
But I don't understand why you don't talk.
Is there something you are hiding beneath that mask,
Are you afraid , people will judge you for who you are?
Why don't you talk to your dear ones,
Is it because you are afraid to face the world?
I don't know how to comfort you,
But you'll have to face the world really soon.

Universe A Mystery

We think we know everything about where we live,
But universe itself is a mystery.
The moment we think we discovered it all,
It's the moment we don't even know about its half.

With millions of stars and the light all around,
It even has blackhole about which we even don't know
now.
The universe is suprise in itself,
But how we are discovering it, is even more suprising than
that.

She

For everyone who thought she was a freak,
And for everyone who said she can't be me.,
Were all jealous of what she had
And wanted to frame her as someone bad.

She smiled everytime at their stupidity
And said everyone, they had some misunderstanding.
But, she wasn't what she looked like.
She was different with her own vibe.

She wasn't scared of anyone's threat,
Nor she was jealous of what other's had.
She was light for people who need help,
And she was satisfied with what she had.

For everyone who thought she was a freak,
And for everyone who said she can't be me.,
Later realised they were wrong,
As she was a real life Queen.

Wildflower

Just like a wildflower,
I want to grow at my odds,
And stand so strong that no one has thought.

Just like a wildflower,
I want to represent joy.
Just like it,
I want to stay firm in life.

Sea

I want to visit sea one day.
I want to travel its shore long way.
I want to see the sunset , while sitting on the sand.
I want to feel the breeze calming my senses.
I want to surf on its tide.
And in night I want to see the reflection of moon from the sky.
I want to preserve that memory in my heart and a box,
And throw that box in the sea, so it can never forget who I was

I Hope

I hope to meet you again, on the crossroads of fate.
Under one umbrella in the rainy day.
I hope to enjoy every moment of life with you,
And when I cry I need your shoulder too.

If I lose my way again,
I hope you to guide me through that phase.
They say all encounters are reunions in disguise,
And I hope destiny to be by my side this time.

Remember

You are rare, and that's what I want you to know.
In the world which is dark and cold ,
Remember you are your own light of hope.

You are attractive, with your own beauty.
And never let anyone's words make you feel guilty.
You are amazing, just the way you are,
And never force yourself to be like some random star.

What I want you to know is that,
You are beautiful with your own heart.

Faith In Life

No matter how hard life creates trouble for you,
All you have to do is try not to lose faith.

Never lose faith in your life,
Because if you lose faith, all you'll have is just regret.

Life is both heaven and hell.
The choice is yours what you want it to play.

Even when life is dark,
You can still shine like a star ,because of light inside you
which is vast.

Clouds

I see the clouds as they pass by,
All different in their own style.

They pass away as the time in our life,
Reminding us to forget what's behind.

The Banyan Tree

The Banyan Tree that stood firm
In the night and even in the sun,
Had seen many things in its lifetime,
People sitting under it and school buses in the daytime.

But now its gone forever
With the wind which passed by.
Now that place has no shade,
Where tree was alive.
And people do not stop there anymore,
They just pass by.

At My Side

In the market which trades
In gold and class,
I had my currency called
Loyalty and a Heart.

In a kingdom of crystal and ice,
All I had was courage to fight.
In darkness no one was at my side,
So I taught myself how to be brave at that time.

Set Free

Don't cry for me, as I was just set free.
I can see you all from here,
I am in a world where angels live.
They don't judge nor they criticise,
They just help souls who were good even at worst times.
Don't cry for me, as I was just set free.
Now I am in a world,
Where I feel happy.

Classroom

Everyone in class teaches you something.
Some teaches you what betrayal feels like,
While some teaches the value of true friendship.

All first benchers are nerds is just an illusion and
All back benchers are problematic is just a misconception.
And all teachers do not treat everyone equally,
With some they are strict while with some they are
friendly.

Middle benchers are all average is just not true.
Some are even toppers,
Though, they differ in attitude.

Every student is unique in their own way,
And that's what makes a classroom a special place.

To Love and to Lose

They say to fall in love is beautiful
But how can I love ,
When I am scared of falling.

The first love story which I know is tragic.
The king is dead,
Leaving alone queen.

How can I love
When I am not capable to trust.
But I want to trust someone who trusts me someday.

I also want to love,but
I am waiting for someone
Who is ready to accept me with all my flaws everyday.

You are a Girl

You are a girl, sit tight
Don't cross your legs its not right.
You are a girl, do the chores
Don't talk back its impolite.
Wear certain clothes, don't go out at night.
You are a girl
Just follow all the rules and you will have a perfect life.
Leave your books and learn to cook.
Don't play sports its not right.

Just because I am a girl have I lost right over my life,
Why should I let some judgemental people
define who am I.

First Snow

Let me live until the first snow comes.
Give me time to say goodbye to my loved ones.
I have a incurable condition and great feelings such as
happiness, sadness and even love can de dangerous.,
That's what doctor said to me
before saying he can't do anything.
I have dyed my fingernails with flower juice,
I am waiting for the first snow to hit my window sometime
soon.

Herself

Emotions became poetry
As a bird was set free—
To be herself.

Memories

People may go but memories live
not for today or tomorrow,
But for eternity.
Some are bad and some are good.
Memories are all that tells us, what
we have gone through.

Memories can hurt and even reminds us of what,
we have done wrong or right.
But some memories of the past, and fear of an innocent
child,
I have thrown it all away into the ocean with the keys
which you can never find.

Notes

Dear readers,

In our life we all have a time when we don't know what to do or where to go. We find ourselves in a situation where we feel all alone. In those times , I want you all to never lose hope or commit the unthinkable. Remember this time will also pass and the better version of yourself is waiting for you ahead.

Sometimes the road of our lives can be seen winding, and you might even get lost along the way, but with the right decision you will always find your destination.

Remember experiencing loss is a part of life, but good things come too.

Life may not give us all the gifts we were hoping for but,

The real gift is life itself .